DON'T CUT THE BASIL

Five Generations of Authentic Italian Recipes

Corrina, Angela, and Mary

Don't Cut the Basil: Five Generations of Authentic Italian Recipes

Pensiero Press

http://www.PensieroPress.com

https://Twitter.com/DrCherylLentz
https://www.Facebook.com/Dr.Cheryl.Lentz
https://www.Linkedin.com/in/drcheryllentz/
https://www.Youtube.com/drcheryllentz
https://www.Instagram.com/drcheryllentz/

Email: drcheryllentz@gmail.com

All rights reserved. No part of this book may be reproduced or transmitted in any form or by any means, graphic, electronic, or mechanical, including photocopying, recording, taping, Web distribution, or by any informational storage and retrieval system without written permission from the publisher except for the inclusion of brief quotations in a review or scholarly reference.

Books are available through Pensiero Press at special discounts for bulk purchases for the purpose of sales promotion, seminar attendance, or educational purposes.

Copyright © 2020 by Pensiero Press

Cover and interior design by Gary Rosenberg • www.thebookcouple.com

Printed in the United States of America

Contents

Foreword   vii

Introduction   1

About the Authors   3

15 Tips We Learned Across the Generations   7

General Health Information   9

EAT IT WHILE IT'S HOT: MAIN DISHES

Angela's Pasta Sauce   12

Mamacita's Italian Meat Sauce   14

Angela's Meatballs   16

Mamacita's Meatballs   18

Mamacita's Pasta e Formaggio   20

Mamacita's San Giuseppe Pasta   22

Mamacita's Tuna Pasta   24

Mamacita's Taco Pasta   26

Nonna Josie's Sicilian Pizza Crust   28

Angela's Italian Wedding Soup   30

IT SMELLS READY: SIDE DISHES & APPETIZERS

Mamacita's Caprese Salad   34

Mamacita's Olive Dip   36

Aunt Angie's Cheese Ball   38

Mamacita's Pecan Cheese Ball   40

Mamacita's Sicilian Olive Salad   42

Watermelon Caprese Inspired by Ale Gambini   44

Corrina's Famous (Party-Favorite) Pepperoni Roll   46

Cugine Bruschetta   48

Angela's Fall Pomegranate Bruschetta   50

Aunt Angie's Amaretto Sweet Potatoes   52

Mamacita's Thanksgiving Stuffing   54

Corrina's Caponata Siciliana   56

ENJOY EVERY BITE: DESSERTS

Nonna Mary's Italian Biscotti   60

Aunt Angie's Carrot (or Zucchini) Cake   62

Mary's Strawberry Granita (Italian Ice)   64

Angela's Cannoli Dip   66

Mary's Bella Luna Cookie   68

Measurements & Conversion Charts   71

Our Genealogy   72

The three of us dedicate this book to our Sicilian heritage, where our great grandparents originated from Palermo, Sicily. We pride ourselves on our food, our hard work, and diverse culture.

☆ ☆ ☆ ☆

We would like to dedicate this cookbook to our grandmother Josephine Arcara Vecchio (Nonna Josie) and our mother Angela Vecchio Siciliano (Aunt Angie). They showed their love through food and recipes, which they shared with many family and friends. We have many memories of our grandmother throwing flour on the kitchen table and teaching us how to make pasta. Our stay-at-home mother spent her time in the kitchen daily cooking and teaching us her recipes. We learned to cook from her by look, taste, and smell. Although our mother is no longer physically with us, we carry on her cooking traditions using the same ingredients, and most of all, cooking with love. ❤

—Angela and Corrina

I dedicate this cookbook to my grandmother (Nonna Mary) and mother Josephine (Mamacita), wonderful examples of love and kindness. My grandmother would often give advice, reminding everyone to chew their food and enjoy their meal, to say their prayers and be thankful for what they have, to save their money, feed the birds, and respect the elderly. What a blessing to be her namesake. Nonna Mary and her siblings were a perfect example of unconditional love, which was clearly passed down and demonstrated by my mother and her siblings. Thank you for sharing it with us. ❤

—Mary

Cugine in Cucina would like to recognize and thank: Carmela McNall for several photographs within this cookbook, particularly on the cover; Troy McNall for his time and patience creating our nutrition labels; Frank Cruz for developing our website and logo.

Foreword

Those who know me well, know how much my maternal grandmother has been fundamental—not only in my work, but in my life. This book is a celebration of grandmothers who, like mine, were the beacon to follow. Through food they taught us much more than cooking; they taught us about life. Although there are differences between Italian and Italian-American cuisine, we all put love into every recipe.

Angela, Corrina, and Mary have collected five generations of family recipes, opening their hearts to readers and honoring their origins and roots.

With this book, readers will be able to take a journey through history, learn classic Italian-American dishes, from Angela's Pasta Sauce, to Nonna Josie's Sicilian Pizza Crust, to Mary's Granita (Italian shaved ice). I'm also flattered to have inspired one of the starters included in the Sides and Appetizers section: Watermelon Caprese Salad.

I'm sure this book will take you back to Sunday dinners when the whole family gathered for hours around the table at grandma's house. Food is a wonderful way to connect people, to build memories, to express a lot of affection. As I always say, FOOD IS LOVE, and in this book, the love of Angela, Corrina, and Mary for their families is deep and tangible.

Buon Appetito!
Ale Gambini
aqueeninthekitchen.com

Introduction

We are so excited to share our family recipes with your family! These recipes include multiple generations of Italian family traditions. They are simple and authentic, and some have been Americanized over time due to the availability of ingredients and resources. Some recipes evolved with each families' taste; therefore, we include varying versions for you to enjoy. Our grandmothers and mothers taught us to cook without measuring, so we use quanto basta (qb), meaning "just enough" throughout this cookbook. If you like more of a particular ingredient, feel free to add it. All temperatures listed in this cookbook are in Fahrenheit. Note: a Centigrade conversion chart can be found on page 71.

Our grandmothers were raised on the most important ingredient—love. They shared that with their daughters who shared that with each of us. Their mother, our great grandmother, bore 10 children in 16 years, but unfortunately she passed away at the young age of 44. Our grandmothers (and their siblings) had a tough life—leaving school to raise the younger children and running a household. Growing up during the Great Depression, this strong sisterhood (along with their brothers) remained close through their 80s and 90s. They taught us to share, love, and give. They truly cared for one another—cooking and baking for family parties, showing up at all of our events, and teaching us about the importance of family. For that, we are forever grateful and blessed to be a part of this family lineage.

We reconnected when Nonna Mary passed away at 96 years young. She was the last of her siblings to pass. Since then, we've been sharing, making, and reinventing family recipes, and now we want to share them with you. To keep our mothers', grandmothers', and great grandmother's traditions alive, we are honored to bring you this cookbook.

www.cugineincucina.com

About the Authors

ANGELA

Angela Siciliano is a home cook. Growing up she was taught to cook traditional Italian meals at home, never eating out. She has many memories spent in the kitchen with her grandmother cooking and listening to stories on how her great grandmother would do things. Angela's biggest influence and teacher was her mother.

Angela's mother taught her the true Italian way to cook—by look, taste, smell, and love—which is never formally measuring but using the senses to know when things are ready. In the Italian culture, food is love! Italians cook and share large amounts of food with friends, family, and anyone that may visit.

Angela redesigns recipes making them her own by using this technique of her senses, from how she was taught. She is now passing her family's traditional Italian cooking on to her two daughters. Research finds that people who eat home-cooked meals on a regular basis tend to be happier, healthier, and live longer lives.

Angela has a passion for health and fitness. She is an American Council on Exercise (ACE) certified instructor a 200-hour Registered Yoga Teacher (RYT) and owns her own business - Adapted Fitness and Yoga Plus, LLC. Angela's business primarily focuses on fitness for individuals with disabilities and their families. Angela also started a YouTube channel (Adapted Fitness and Yoga Plus) where she shares fitness videos and short cooking lessons.

Angela is excited to share her traditional family recipes along with the ones she's created. She invites everyone that loves family, Italian food, and traditions to cook with her.

For more information on Adapted Fitness please visit her **website: www.adaptedfyp.com** or **email: adaptedfyp@gmail.com**

CORRINA

Corrina learned to cook at home from her mother. Growing up in an all-Italian family, waking up on Sunday morning smelling her mother's sauce on the stove was a weekly family tradition. Corrina would stand in the kitchen and watch her mother add all the ingredients into a large sauce pan to simmer all day long. Since her mother didn't measure anything, she remembers frequently being asked to "check the sauce on the stove" by taking a spoon and tasting it to determine if anything needed to be added. Sundays meant being in the kitchen all day with much anticipation for a large pasta dinner with sausage and meatballs.

Corrina remembers when her grandmother threw flour in the middle of the kitchen table and said, "Let me show you how we make homemade dough!" Cooking traditions have been something that have been passed down as her grandmother would share stories about her mother and sisters, and how they would cook Italian foods and desserts. She was taught how to make her famous pepperoni roll and homemade pizzas from her mother, who would make them for all her birthday parties throughout her childhood. She remembers her friends always excited to come over for dinner, knowing they were getting a homemade Italian meal. Now, Corrina is always asked to make her pepperoni roll when she is invited to any events, and it's still a party favorite! Growing up, any special occasions, holidays, and even funerals have always been centered around Italian food. Corrina was taught that this is how you show love, support, and sympathy to others—through the love of food.

As an avid marathon and ultra-marathon runner, Corrina takes advantage of what she learned from her grandmother and mother. She takes her pasta and pizza cooking skills to create carb-loaded meals to fuel for her runs and shares those with friends in the running community. Corrina earned her BA from Baldwin Wallace University. As a certified Project Management Professional (PMP) and working in the corporate financial industry for over 20 years, she continues to share recipes with co-workers and friends, who always look to add traditional Italian meals to their lives.

MARY

Mary learned to make family recipes from her mother and grandmother. As a young girl, Mary loved being in the kitchen tasting the freshly made sauce, smelling the cookies baking in the oven, or waiting for the next taste test. When cooking or baking, Nonna Mary used to ask Mary to sing or whistle. Mary learned later in life that it wasn't to hear her (beautiful?) singing voice, but that Nonna Mary did this to be sure Mary wasn't eating the ingredients! Nonna Mary was an amazing baker.

Two favorite memories of Mary's are Sunday family dinners and Christmas Eve. Sunday dinners were a family favorite that her mother carried on for years—fresh sauce cooking all day, fresh Italian bread, homemade meatballs and sausage, different types of pastas... The entire family would come over and sit around the kitchen table for hours. Every Christmas Eve the older generation carried on the tradition of the seven fishes, and there would be a kitchen full of different types of homemade pizzas. We would crowd around the table and enjoy one another's company.

Mary has her Ph.D. from Miami University, MBA from Cleveland State University, and BA from Baldwin Wallace University; she has numerous publications and has earned multiple awards. She is a tenured university professor and also a contributor to *In the Limelight* and *ItalyUSA* magazines. Mary is also the owner of Ciao Down Italian Cookies, LLC, a side business she started in honor of her grandmother.

She is a proud member of the Order Sons and Daughters of Italy in America (OSDIA); Mary serves as a co-host on the Facebook series "OSDIA Interviews LIVE" where she had the pleasure of interviewing amazing Italian and Italian American chefs including Lidia Bastianich, Mary Ann Esposito, Ale Gambini, and Cara Di Falco. Additionally, she was asked by Ale Gambini to write a review for her new cookbook. For the Order, she serves in multiple roles nationally, for the Grand Lodge of Ohio, and locally. Additionally, her mother was quoted a number of times in the *Cleveland Memories* book series, sharing stories of her Italian upbringing.

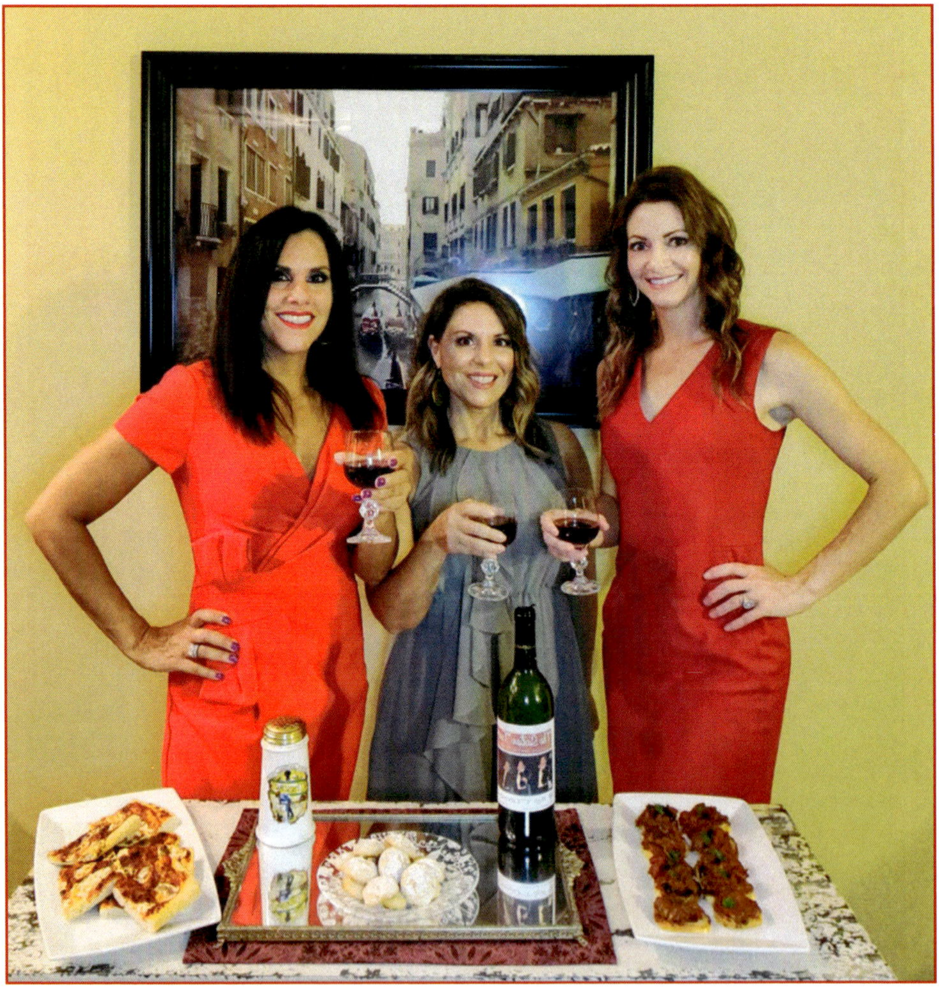

15 Tips We Learned Across the Generations

1. Have a clean, prepared working space with ingredients and tools ready to go prior to starting any recipe.
2. As Nonna Mary always said, never leave the kitchen when the oven is on or if something is cooking on the stovetop.
3. Regardless of how well your garbage disposal works, never put pasta or a dry flour-like mixture in it. It will create a paste and cause many issues in the future.
4. Egg likes egg, not your finger. After cracking so many dozens of eggs, once in a while a piece of the shell falls into the bowl. Egg likes egg. Use a sturdy part of the shell (without the risk of other pieces breaking) to scoop out the fallen piece.
5. Mamacita says that when you add spices, you will know when you have the right amount by how it smells. Look, taste, and smell—then you'll know it's ready!
6. Read through each recipe prior to beginning. You'll feel more prepared and will be less likely to miss a tip.
7. If you ever over-toast bread, use a butter knife to scrape off the deep brown crust. It will still taste just as good!
8. Always get a new spoon to taste your food, and never eat over the main dish!
9. Always tie your hair back whenever you are making anything in the kitchen. *Always.*
10. Always start with cold water before boiling water.

11. Always put pasta noodles in brown sugar to keep it from forming hard clumps.
12. Never, ever rinse your noodles! The sauce is less likely to stick, even if it's a rigate noodle.
13. Never cut your basil, only tear it. It's just the right thing to do.
14. Don't salt the mushrooms until after you cook them. If you salt while sautéing, they just get soggy. And wipe them clean rather than rinsing them, or they could get rubbery.
15. Never waste food. Mary's grandmother instilled this in her. No matter what, do what you can to never waste it. If you have cookies that are getting a little hard, break them up and feed the crumbs to the birds; if you have leftovers or fresh ingredients that need to be used and can't be frozen, chop them up and add them to a pasta, soup, salad, or other main dish so you don't waste any food.

General Health Information

NUTRITIONAL LABELS

We know many people have special diets, and we thought it would be helpful to include nutritional labels for each of our recipes. We want to disclose that we are not nutritionists but used an app to obtain the nutritional information that we share for you. Labels for each of our recipes can be found on our website—**www.cugineincucina.com**.

GLUTEN SENSITIVE RECIPES

Gluten is found in grains and wheats, most often in flour and the doughs of traditional pasta dishes. Most cream cheese, butter, margarine, and shortenings are gluten free, unless other flavors are infused, which could include gluten. In this cookbook, the recipes below contain no grains or wheats.

    Please note: The recipes denoted with an asterisk (*) include seasonings such as onion and/or garlic powders that may contain a filler with gluten and should be excluded for those with gluten sensitivities.

1. Angela's Pasta Sauce*
2. Mamacita's Italian Meat Sauce*
3. Mamacita's Caprese Salad
4. Mamacita's Olive Dip
5. Aunt Angie's Cheese Ball
6. Mamacita's Pecan Cheese Ball
7. Watermelon Caprese
8. Aunt Angie's Amaretto Sweet Potatoes
9. Angela's Cannoli Dip
10. Mary's Strawberry Granita

Additionally, the following dishes can be made by using a gluten-free pasta:

1. Mamacita's San Guiseppe Pasta*
2. Mamacita's Tuna Pasta*

    Unfortunately, Mamacita's Sicilian Olive Salad is not gluten-free because it contains rice vinegar. However, eliminating rice vinegar as an ingredient would be fine, not dramatically changing the taste of the salad.

EAT IT WHILE IT'S HOT: MAIN DISHES

Angela's Pasta Sauce (serves 6–8)

The traditional Italian family pasta sauce... Angela spent many Sundays in the kitchen learning to make her family's pasta sauce from her mother, who was taught from Angela's grandmother, who learned it from our great grandmother. Now Angela is teaching her own daughters this family recipe. This is so flavorful, just add it to your favorite pasta! FUN FACT: Angela, Corrina, and Mary's Great Aunt Dolly (their grandmothers' sister) added red wine to her sauce.

INGREDIENTI

- 1 18-oz. can tomato paste
- 1 14.5-oz. can diced tomatoes with basil, garlic, and oregano
- 1 T garlic powder
- 2 T dried basil
- 2 tsp dried oregano
- 1 tsp salt (add more to taste)
- 1 medium Spanish onion

Direzioni

- Add tomato paste and 3 cans of water (use tomato paste can to measure water) into a pot on high heat and stir.
- Add the diced tomatoes and spices, stir well.
- Drop in the whole onion (peeled).
- Bring the sauce to a boil. Once boiling, turn down heat to low and simmer for 1 hour, stirring about every 10 minutes.
- After an hour, taste the sauce.
- Add any spices to taste as needed.
- Continue to simmer on low for another 1–2 hours.

Note

The sauce tastes better the longer it simmers, but it can be enjoyed after 1 hour.

Tip

Always salt the water generously before boiling your pasta! It's the only chance you get to season it!

EAT IT WHILE IT'S HOT: MAIN DISHES

Mamacita's Italian Meat Sauce
(makes 4–5 gallons)

A family favorite for sure! This sauce was served not only during holidays and family gatherings, but nearly every Sunday for our family dinners—and everyone was invited! Mamacita kept her family's tradition of large Sunday gatherings for many decades. Now, extended family and friends of her children are making this sauce for their own families!

INGREDIENTI

- 2 105-oz. cans tomato sauce
- 2 6-oz. cans tomato paste
- 12 count sweet Italian sausage
- 1 large package country boneless ribs (pork)
- Water for pots
- 1 T garlic powder
- 2 tsp basil
- 1 T oregano
- 1 T salt (add more to taste)
- 1 T parsley

Direzioni

- Cut each of the sausage links in half, creating 24 pieces.
- In two very large pots, add both the sausage pieces and the ribs, then pour enough water to cover the sausages and ribs.
- Boil for 30 minutes (meat will fully cook).
- Add the sauce, paste, and seasonings.
- Then, simply cook for 2 hours on a slow boil.
- Stir occasionally to avoid sauce burning on the bottom of the pot.
- Taste throughout the process, as you please!
- After 2 hours, turn the oven off and let it sit for another 2 hours.
- This is the point where we separate the meat from the actual sauce. We put the meat in a different bowl, which allows people to select whether they would like to include ribs and/or sausage with their meal, or just enjoy this mouthwatering sauce.
- Serve warm (usually with pasta) and store in the refrigerator. The sauce will freeze well.

EAT IT WHILE IT'S HOT: MAIN DISHES

Angela's Meatballs
(serves 8+)

Angela's meatball recipe was inspired from watching her mother make them when she was a young girl growing up in Cleveland. She remembers being 6 or 7 years old, standing next to her mom in the kitchen while she made her meatballs. Since she never used recipes, Angela learned the traditional Italian way—by watching, smelling, and looking at the amount of ingredients going into the bowl, then enjoying a taste test! She wrote this recipe for everyone who loves Italian food but needs an easy recipe to follow. These are all the ingredients her mother taught her to use and exactly how she makes her meatballs today.

INGREDIENTI

- 1 lb. ground pork
- 1 lb. ground beef from chuck
- 1 egg
- ¼ cup Italian seasoned bread crumbs
- 1½ tsp salt
- 1 tsp fresh ground pepper
- 2 fresh garlic cloves minced
- 2 tsp dried basil
- 1 tsp dried oregano
- 1½ T fresh Italian parsley finely chopped
- 2 T ground parmigiana cheese

Direzioni

- At room temperature, mix the meat and all other ingredients by hand in a large mixing bowl.
- Roll meatballs into 2-inch balls and place on oven-safe baking tray.
- Preheat oven to 350°F.
- Bake for 40 minutes. Or, cook meatballs for 25 minutes then let simmer in the pasta sauce for at least 45 minutes or longer.

EAT IT WHILE IT'S HOT: MAIN DISHES   17

Mamacita's Meatballs
(makes ~20 meatballs)

Mamacita made thousands of these meatballs over the years. They can be frozen to eat at a later time. Mary substitutes lean ground turkey for the ground beef and flavors with a little more of the same spices. They are rolled to about the size of a female adult's fist and are great with your favorite pasta dish or to make the best meatball sandwich you ever had!

INGREDIENTI

- 1 lb. ground beef
- ¾ cup Italian seasoned bread crumbs
- ¼ cup grated pecorino Romano cheese
- 2 eggs
- 1 tsp garlic powder
- 1 tsp salt
- 1 tsp parsley
- ½ tsp pepper
- 2 T olive oil

Direzioni

- In a mixer, add the bread crumbs and pecorino Romano grated cheese.
- Add the spices and mix the dry ingredients well.
- Add the eggs and mix.
- Add the ground beef and mix well.
- Once mixed, remove from mixer and put in large mixing bowl.
- Coat the frying pan with light layer of oil.
- Fill a small bowl with water.
- Grab a small fistful of the meatball mix and lightly dip in water.
- Roll the meat mixture into a ball using a circular motion with both palms of your hands. Place and arrange each meatball in the pan.
- When the pan is filled with ready-to-cook meatballs, turn the stovetop on medium heat and cover.
- Flip the meatballs when the bottoms are lightly brown. Continue to flip and move them accordingly, until meatballs brown to your liking. Add water to the pan if they begin to stick.
- Serve warmed; refrigerate for leftovers.

EAT IT WHILE IT'S HOT: MAIN DISHES

Mamacita's Pasta e Formaggio
(serves 8+)

This is arguably the best Italian version of the traditional American macaroni and cheese. Often times Mamacita would slice fresh tomatoes across the top prior to baking. We usually use elbow-shaped pasta, but cellentani is another favorite. As an alternative to breadcrumbs, sprinkle Italian spices over the tomato slices and a few shakes of garlic salt and pepper to top off this dish. It was a staple growing up in our household!

INGREDIENTI

- 1 lb. elbow pasta
- 18 oz. of sharp cheddar cheese (in a block)
- 3½ cups of milk
- ⅓ cup of flour
- ¼ cup butter (½ stick)
- ¾ cup Italian bread crumbs
- 2 T olive oil
- Sale e pepe (qb)

Direzioni

- Boil the pasta according to the instructions.
- Warm the milk on the stovetop and add flour (low-to-medium heat). Stir until thick.
- Add the butter and mix until it melts into the sauce.
- When all ingredients are combined and thick, add the cheese. **TIP:** Cut the cheese into small pieces so it melts faster.
- When the cheese melts, it will look like a smooth cheese sauce. For a thicker sauce, use ½ cup of flour.
- After draining the pasta, add melted cheese sauce to pasta in an oven-safe dish.
- In a separate bowl, mix the bread crumbs and the olive oil.
- Layer the top of the pasta with bread crumb mix before placing it in the oven (do not cover).
- Bake on 350°F for 35–45 minutes (depending on shape of dish) or until the sides start to golden.
- Before serving, sprinkle with salt and pepper to your liking.
- Salad is usually served after or with this meal.

EAT IT WHILE IT'S HOT: MAIN DISHES

Mamacita's San Giuseppe Pasta
(serves 4–6)

This is a twist on your traditional pasta dish. It bursts with flavor and like all pasta, is just as good or better the next day! Remembering how Nonna and her sisters survived the Great Depression—they often made do with what they had in their cupboards—we used that same mindset. We celebrated St. Joseph's day in the 2020 quarantine with this fantastic dish, and it has since become another family favorite!

FUN FACT: Nonna Josie was born on St Joseph's day and named Giuseppa in honor of this feast day!

INGREDIENTI

1 lb. short pasta

1½ cups grape tomatoes

1 cup green olives

1 large onion

2-3 cloves of garlic (qb)

1 tsp Italian seasoning

Olive oil (qb)

Sale e pepe (qb)

Onion powder (qb)

Direzioni

- Boil the water for your favorite short pasta according to the instructions (e.g. rigatoni, rotini, medium shells, gemelli, etc.).
- While the pasta is boiling, cut both the olives and grape tomatoes in half.
- Sauté the onions, garlic, and grape tomatoes together on the stovetop.
- Make pasta as directed.
- After draining the pasta, add the sautéed onions, garlic, and grape tomatoes.
- Add the Italian seasoning, onion powder, salt, pepper, and olive oil to taste.
- Mix well and serve warm.

EAT IT WHILE IT'S HOT: MAIN DISHES

Mamacita's Tuna Pasta
(serves 8+)

Warning—This pasta dish is addicting! We usually use tricolor farfalle or cellentani pasta for this dish in particular. It is such a fresh-tasting pasta meal, and it is perfect for outdoor picnics. It can be served warm, at room temperature, or cool. Mamacita's father, Joe, would make this for their family regularly, especially in the hot summer months growing up in Cleveland. Whether they were going to a picnic or someone was just visiting, this was always a staple dish in the house.

INGREDIENTI

- 1 lb. short pasta (cellentani used here)
- 2 7-oz. cans of tuna
- ½ large onion
- 2 long celery stalks
- ¼ cup olive oil
- Zest of 1 lemon
- Squeezed juice from both zested lemons
- Sale e pepe (qb)
- Onion powder (qb)
- Garlic powder (qb)

Direzioni

- Boil the pasta according to the instructions.
- Cut the celery stalks and onion. The pieces of the celery and onion should be about the same size as the short pasta or a little smaller.
- In a large bowl, add the celery and onion.
- After draining the pasta, add it to the bowl of onion and celery.
- Zest 1 whole lemon, then cut lemon in half and squeeze the juice in the bowl. Be sure to keep the seed-side up (then you're less likely to get seeds in the bowl).
- Add the olive oil and mix well.
- Dust a light layer of onion powder and garlic powder across the top (qb).
- Sprinkle salt and pepper to taste.
- Mix well before serving.
- Store in refrigerator.
- Serve chilled. Add salt and pepper if you please.

EAT IT WHILE IT'S HOT: MAIN DISHES

Mamacita's Taco Pasta
(serves 8+)

Taco Tuesday became a movement during the 2020 world-wide quarantine. Mamacita Italianized it! We used farfalle for this meal, but rotini or cavatelli would be good pasta to use as well. It became a fun twist on pasta during tough times, similar to how Nonna Mary would cater her pastas to what she had in the pantry for her own family during the Great Depression.

INGREDIENTI

1 lb. short pasta

1 cup corn

16 oz. ground turkey

1 medium onion

1 small can diced tomatoes

1 cup grated cheddar cheese

Taco seasoning, 1 packet

1 T olive oil to fry meat

1 can of tomato sauce (optional)

Sale & pepe (qb)

Direzioni

- Boil the pasta according to the instructions.
- Mix the taco seasoning with ground turkey and brown in a frying pan.
- Chop, then sauté onions while turkey is browning.
- Steam the corn (or microwave if you please).
- When the pasta is drained, put in large bowl. Add the ground turkey and sautéed onions.
- Add the corn and drained diced tomatoes to pasta dish.
- Mix well.
- Once plated, serve with grated cheddar cheese (add more to taste) and salt and pepper (qb).

Variations

Serve over romaine lettuce rather than pasta. Add black beans accordingly.

EAT IT WHILE IT'S HOT: MAIN DISHES

Nonna Josie's Sicilian Pizza Crust
(makes 2 9" x 14" pizzas)

The sisters, our grandmothers, all made their own homemade pizza. Mary and Corrina have similar memories growing up and walking into their grandparents' home. The warm smell of the freshly made dough, then the sauce... Coincidentally, they both remember being just tall enough to see over the table and not allowed to eat anything quite yet! Nonna Mary made her homemade pizza regularly, but the most popular tradition included her many homemade pizzas with thick crust every Christmas Eve with toppings such as sausage, pepperoni, peppers, onions, mushrooms, and a variety cheeses dusted on top—in addition to the seven fishes, of course!

Angela has memories of the pizza trays lined up in the breezeway at their grandmother's house with the kitchen towels draped over all of the rising pizza doughs.

Both our grandmothers used rectangle baking sheets to make their pizzas, but you can also use a pizza stone. Angela and Corrina have since enhanced their grandmother's pizza dough recipe and make it for their own families.

INGREDIENTI

1 package dry yeast

2 tsp sugar

2 ¼ cups cold water

5 cups flour

1 ½ tsp salt

Nonstick spray

1 T olive oil

Direzioni

- In mixer with dough hook, combine all dry ingredients. Start the mixer on low and add water.
- Mix on low for about 7 minutes; the dough will start to form into a ball.
- Spray a large bowl (or plastic wrap) with nonstick spray.
- Pay attention to the dough—If the dough is still a bit sticky, add a little more flour and mix another minute or two.
- Remove the dough, form into a ball, and place onto the plastic wrap or into a bowl. Rub the dough with olive oil. Cover the dough with a clean kitchen towel and let rise for an hour.

- Spread the dough, forming the pizza onto a lightly greased pizza pan, cookie sheet, or if using a pizza stone, onto parchment paper, until dough is about ½-inch thick. Your pizza can be rectangular or round.

- Cover the dough again with a clean kitchen towel and let it rise for another hour or two before adding toppings of your choice.

- Pre-heat the oven to 500°F and bake for 14–16 minutes.

- If using a pizza stone, cook the pizza about halfway, then remove the parchment paper to get an extra crispy crust. When the pizza comes out of the oven, immediately brush the crust with olive oil.

TIP: Make the dough a day or two early and keep it in the refrigerator wrapped tightly in both plastic wrap and a 1-gallon ziplock bag. You can also freeze the dough right away for up to 3 months.

Angela's Italian Wedding Soup
(serves 9)

Angela tasted many other Italian wedding soups made over the years, but she was never really impressed by any of them. Nearly a decade ago, she started making her own homemade wedding soup. This soup is so filled with flavor! The combination of meatballs, pasta, chicken, and other ingredients soothe your soul.

INGREDIENTI

3 lbs. chicken

Mini meatballs

2 48-oz. cans of chicken stock

Water for large pot

Chicken-flavored soup base (to taste)

1 lb. Italian Escarole or Baby Spinach (qb)

Dried basil, oregano, garlic powder & pinch seasoned salt (qb)

1 box pastina or ditalini pasta

Direzioni

NOTE: Use bone-in chicken thighs or use split chicken breast, Angela's Meatball Recipe under Main Dishes, and use chopped escarole or baby spinach.

- Pour chicken stock and water into a large pot, filling it about ¾ full. Bring the liquid to a boil and add in the chicken. Boil approximately 25 minutes, or until the chicken is cooked through.

- While the chicken is boiling, make mini Italian meatballs (1/2–1 inch round).

- When chicken is cooked, remove the chicken and shred.

- Add the mini meatballs into the boiling broth and water to cook for about 20 minutes. If the liquid starts getting low, add more water and bring it back up to a boil.

- Add the dried basil, oregano, garlic powder, and a little seasoned salt (all qb). Stir in chicken-flavored soup base, adding a spoonful at a time until the broth is to your liking.

- Add back the shredded chicken into pot.

- Add the chopped Italian escarole or baby spinach.

- Make pastina or ditalini pasta according to the box directions. Add pasta to each bowl and pour the wedding soup over the top.

Tips

1. Serve with fresh roasted garlic and Italian bread.
2. To save some time, you can use roasted rotisserie chicken.
3. For a little extra flavor, sprinkle some grated Parmesan cheese on your freshly served soup!

Helpful Hint

To roast garlic, buy 2–4 large fresh garlic bulbs and cut off the top of the garlic bulb until all cloves are exposed. Place the garlic bulb into a piece of tin foil. Season the garlic with salt and pepper. Drizzle a good amount of olive oil over the top. Wrap the garlic bulb inside the tin foil, twisting it at the top so it resembles a garlic bulb. Roast in a pre-heated oven at 450°F for 45 minutes. Squeeze out the roasted garlic and spread onto Italian bread.

IT SMELLS READY: SIDE DISHES & APPETIZERS

Mamacita's Caprese Salad
(serves 4-6)

This is one of our summertime favorites! With only three ingredients and no cooking, anyone can make this! It can be made ahead of time and stored in the refrigerator, covered with plastic wrap. These ingredients were picked fresh from our garden. The key to this display is that all ingredients are all cut about the same size and arranged in a pattern. You can adjust the thickness of the tomatoes or mozzarella to your liking. You know it's good when it looks like the Italian flag!

INGREDIENTI

4 Fresh tomatoes

Fresh basil leaves (qb)

Fresh mozzarella (8 oz.)

Direzioni

- Use equal parts for each ingredient.
- Slice the tomato and mozzarella the same width.
- Arrange these 3 ingredients into a pattern.
- Serve chilled. Add salt and pepper, if you please.

DON'T CUT THE BASIL

IT SMELLS READY: SIDE DISHES & APPETIZERS   35

Mamacita's Olive Dip
(serves 4+)

This is a quick dip to make when company arrives, and of course as Italians, we always offer guests something to eat! This olive dip is made with three ingredients, and there is no cooking involved. It can be made in advance and stored in the refrigerator. Mary's Nonna Estelle first made it years ago and would serve it in a small bowl on a platter surrounded by our favorite crackers, or simply with crackers in a bowl for her messy grandchildren! Now, Mamacita and Mary make this olive dip when they entertain. It can be made in less than 15 minutes, so it's great to serve when you're in a pinch!

INGREDIENTI

1 scant cup green Spanish olives (add more to taste)

2+ T sour cream

8 oz. cream cheese

Crackers

Direzioni

- Slice the olives into pieces—thinly slice them for a mild texture or cut them into chunks for bolder flavor.

- Mash the cream cheese well with a fork in a bowl. It's easier to mash when the cream cheese is at room temperature.

- Add 2 heaping tablespoons of sour cream and mix well. Add more sour cream to taste (qb).

- Mix well and fully incorporate the sliced olives. Taste and add ingredients accordingly. Always add a little, because you can always add more later!

- Store the dip in refrigerator and serve with your favorite salty crackers.

IT SMELLS READY: SIDE DISHES & APPETIZERS 37

Aunt Angie's Cheese Ball
(serves 6+)

Aunt Angie would make this when family was coming over for a holiday gathering. Another no-cook side, it's quick to make and enjoyed by everyone. It can be made ahead of time, kept in the refrigerator, and wrapped in plastic wrap to hold its shape. This was often served on a platter in the shape of a ball, surrounded by Triscuit crackers.

INGREDIENTI

2 8-oz. cream cheese (softened)

¼ lb. Bavarian ham (lean)

1 T yellow onion

½ cup green olives with pimento

Direzioni

- Finely chop the olives, onion, and ham.
- In a mixing bowl, combine the softened cream cheese, olives, onions, and ham. Mix well until everything is combined.
- Place mixture onto a large piece of plastic wrap and form into a ball.
- Unwrap and place on a platter to be served with Triscuit crackers.

IT SMELLS READY: SIDE DISHES & APPETIZERS

Mamacita's Pecan Cheese Ball
(serves 4+)

This was always a favorite appetizer at family parties. Another no-cook side, it can be made ahead of time by storing wrapped in plastic wrap in the refrigerator. This pecan cheese ball is served on a platter encircled by Ritz crackers. The raspberry jam adds the sweetness, mixed with the salty crackers, makes a perfect sweet/savory crunch!

INGREDIENTI

- ½ cup pecans
- 1 cup sharp cheddar cheese (shredded)
- ½ onion (finely chopped)
- 8 oz. cream cheese
- Seedless raspberry jam

Direzioni

- Finely chop the onion and cut pecans into small pieces.
- Mash the cream cheese at room temperature. **TIP:** Cut into smaller rectangles before mixing.
- Add in the chopped pecans, sharp cheddar cheese, and finely chopped onion.
- Mix well. Form into a ball, add pecans to the top for decoration.
- Cover and chill in refrigerator until it is ready to serve.
- Pour raspberry jam around the ball, or pour over the top and let it run over the sides.
- Serve with Ritz crackers.

IT SMELLS READY: SIDE DISHES & APPETIZERS 41

Mamacita's Sicilian Olive Salad
(serves 6+)

Everyone looks forward to this salad when Mamacita makes it! It can be made ahead of time and stored in the refrigerator. It is easiest to serve in a large bowl. Our favorite way to eat it is with fresh sliced Italian bread and slices of mozzarella cheese to accompany the salad. We don't eat the salad on top of the bread/cheese—Mamacita would say that's not very Italian! ☺

INGREDIENTI

Sicilian olives (qb)

Celery (qb)

Cherry tomatoes (qb)

Cucumber (qb)

EVOO (qb)

Rice vinegar (qb)

Oregano (qb)

Garlic powder (qb)

OPTIONAL: Fresh Italian bread and mozzarella cheese (qb)

Direzioni

- Measure the Sicilian olives, celery, cherry tomatoes, and cucumbers into equal parts and cut all to the same size.

RECOMMENDATION: Go a tad lighter on the olives (most expensive) and a little heavier on the celery (least expensive).

- Add for flavor (to taste, qb):
  - Extra virgin olive oil (EVOO)
  - Rice vinegar (a splash)
  - Oregano
  - Garlic powder (light)

Note

The salad will naturally produce a nice juicy flavor. If there is too much EVOO or vinegar, it will overpower the dynamic of the salad.

IT SMELLS READY: SIDE DISHES & APPETIZERS

Watermelon Caprese
Inspired by Ale Gambini (serves 8)

For this recipe, it's easiest to create an assembly line of ingredients. In preparation for Mary's interview with Ale Gambini on the Facebook series OSDIA Interviews LIVE, *she, along with Angela and Corrina, made Ale's version of this flavorful salad.*

They found the zest of the lemon coupled with the balsamic glaze allows the flavors to burst with each bite! The coarse salt dusted over the salad makes this salad unforgettable. Served as a salad or skewers, these are perfect for summer picnics, party appetizers, or afternoon snacks!

INGREDIENTI

1 seedless watermelon

1 bunch fresh basil

8 oz. fresh mozzarella

Zest of 1 lemon

Olive oil (qb)

Balsamic glaze (qb)

Coarse salt (qb)

Skewers/toothpicks

Direzioni

- Cube watermelon.
- On a serving platter or in a large bowl, add watermelon, mozzarella, and basil.
- Sprinkle with coarse salt, drizzle with olive oil and balsamic glaze. Top with lemon zest.

Helpful Hint

Whether you use skewers, toothpicks, or serve as a salad, each should have at least: a small piece of basil, a mozzarella pearl, and a cube of watermelon.

IT SMELLS READY: SIDE DISHES & APPETIZERS   45

Corrina's Famous (Party-Favorite) Pepperoni Roll (serves 6)

Corrina often hosts Sicilian Sundays, holidays, and family parties at her house. When she visits friends, she is often asked to make her famous pepperoni rolls! This delicious combination of cheese and pepperoni will make your guests want more. Once cooled, they are sliced into pieces 1 inch to 2 inches thick. These pepperoni rolls are so easy to make and can be served as an appetizer or with a great pasta dish. Assume 12 slices per roll.

INGREDIENTI

1 lb. pizza dough (room temperature)

1 stick Margarita pepperoni

1 cup shredded mozzarella (or provolone)

Nonstick cooking spray

Direzioni

- Spray a nonstick cooking spray on foil or a baking sheet.
- Work the dough into a rectangle to a thickness of about ½ inch.
- Down the middle (long-ways), cover the dough with pepperoni.
- Cover the pepperoni with the shredded mozzarella (qb).
- Pull the right side of the dough to the middle (or a little over).
- Pull the left side of the dough over the middle (or a little over).
- Secure all of the seams by carefully pinching dough together. This will ensure there aren't any explosions while cooking in the oven.
- Bake at 350°F for 30 minutes or until golden brown.
- When cooled, slice into 1- to 2-inch pieces.
- Store in refrigerator.
- Serve as you please—warm, out of the fridge, or at room temperature.

Note

Other family versions include a light layer of olive oil and Italian seasonings before placing any other ingredients on the dough and glazing with egg wash prior to baking in the oven.

Cugine Bruschetta
(serves 6)

Pronounced with a "K" sound rather than a "sha" sound, this is another great appetizer or complement to any meal. The best tasting bruschetta uses the freshest quality ingredients. You'll want to pay attention to the juiciness of the tomatoes. If they are very juicy, you'll want to serve right away so the bread stays crunchy. When Angela, Corrina, and Mary make these little slices of heaven, they never have leftovers!

INGREDIENTI

6 ripe tomatoes

1 bunch fresh basil

8 oz. fresh mozzarella

1-2 cloves minced garlic

Olive oil (qb)

Balsamic glaze (qb)

Sliced Italian bread, toasted

Direzioni

- Dice each of the tomatoes into small pieces.
- Add the following to your taste (qb):
    - Fresh basil (torn)
    - Fresh mozzarella
    - Minced garlic (to taste)
- Drizzle olive oil.
- Drizzle balsamic glaze.
- Layer the tomato mixture on a toasted Italian bread.
- Serve cold and shortly after making.

IT SMELLS READY: SIDE DISHES & APPETIZERS

Angela's Fall Pomegranate Bruschetta (serves 3)

As fresh ingredients change with the seasons, we thought we would change up the bruschetta! Instead of using tomatoes as a base, we use fresh pomegranate seeds. It makes 6 small appetizers (2 per person).

INGREDIENTI

1½ cup pomegranate seeds (~4 pomegranates)

2 T finely chopped shallot

1 pinch of coarse salt

2 T dark molasses

1 T pomegranate juice (fresh from the pomegranate or from Pom 100% juice)

Fresh mint (qb)

Fresh ricotta cheese (drained)

Honey (qb)

Balsamic glaze (qb)

Thinly sliced Italian bread, toasted

Olive oil (for toasted bread)

Direzioni

- Combine the pomegranate seeds (drained; save juice for later) and shallot in a small bowl.
- In a separate bowl, mix together dark molasses, pomegranate juice, and a pinch of coarse salt.
- Add to pomegranate seeds and shallot, then mix.
- Drizzle olive oil over the bread and toast the bread.
- Assemble the following to your taste (qb):
  - Spread generous amount of ricotta on piece of toasted Italian bread
  - Spoon on pomegranate seed mixture
  - Drizzle balsamic glaze and honey
  - Top with finely topped mint (qb)
- Assemble when ready to plate.

DON'T CUT THE BASIL

Tip

Roll with a heavy hand the fresh pomegranate on the counter to loosen the seeds inside. Cut the pomegranate in half and over a bowl, hit the skin of the pomegranate with the back of a spoon to loosen and drop seeds.

Note

If you prefer goat cheese over ricotta cheese, crumble goat cheese on top of pomegranate seed mixture during assembly—just before adding the glaze and mint.

Aunt Angie's Amaretto Sweet Potatoes (serves 10+)

This portion size was served at many family gatherings, especially during the holidays. Angela and Corrina's mother started making her Amaretto sweet potatoes for Thanksgiving. One year she didn't make the sweet potatoes, and the family loudly gave her so much grief! From that Thanksgiving on, they had been a staple and the only potatoes we have on Thanksgiving. Since their mother's passing in 2009, Angela proudly took over making them every Thanksgiving.

INGREDIENTI

9 large sweet potatoes

1 cup sugar

½ cup honey

1 ½ cups packed brown sugar

½ + ¼ tsp ground ginger

6 T cornstarch

1 cup orange juice

1 cup pineapple juice

3 tsp lemon juice

¾ cup amaretto

6 T butter

1 20-oz. can pineapple tidbits (optional)

1 bag of chopped pecans (optional)

Direzioni

- Preheat oven to 350°F.

TIP: Fork each sweet potato and place right in microwave. Cook 3 at a time, at 5–7 minutes per potato (or just until you can squeeze the sides of each potato easily). Microwave times can vary, especially with the different potato sizes. This process makes them easier to peel & cut!

- Let the potatoes cool, peel and cut into 1- to 2-inch cubes.

- Place the cut sweet potatoes into large casserole dish.

- In a heavy sauce pot, over medium heat, combine the rest of the ingredients except the butter and Amaretto.

- Bring mixture to a boil, stirring frequently with a whisk.

- When the mixture is boiling, add in the butter and Amaretto.

- Once combined, pour mixture over the sweet potatoes and bake in the oven for about 50 minutes, until sauce is thickened.

Optional

After pouring mixture over potatoes, sprinkle pineapple tidbits and chopped pecans over the top before putting into the oven.

Mamacita's Thanksgiving Stuffing (serves 12+)

This recipe is time-consuming to prepare, but worth every minute. It's been made for every Thanksgiving dinner for the last 50+ years in our family. It started when Mary's Great Sia Rosaria played with a family recipe, then Nonna Mary made it, and Mamacita still makes it with some minor enhancements. Similar to Aunt Angie's Amaretto Sweet Potatoes, it's become more important to have this for Thanksgiving than any other item. On average, our Thanksgiving meal consists of about twenty people. This stuffing is just as good the next day, if it lasts that long!

INGREDIENTI

6 bunches celery

5 loaves sliced white bread

12 eggs

3 lbs. Bob Evans bulk sausage

4 large onions—chopped

1 stick of butter

1 carton turkey stock (32 fl. oz.)

Olive oil—to sauté

Direzioni

- Cut the bread into 1-inch squares and set each of the pieces on baking sheets to dry for at least 3–4 hours.
- Sauté the celery in 1 stick of butter.
- Sauté the onions in 1 stick of butter.
- When the bread is dried, put in large mixing bowl.
- Manually break the sausage into pea-sized pieces.
- Mix with bread pieces.
- Beat the eggs in a separate bowl.
- Add the eggs, sautéed onions, and celery to mix.
- Mix well. Divide mixture into two 9" x 13" pans.
- Bake at 350°F for 2 hours or until browned.
- When it is almost done baking (5 or 10 minutes remain), remove from the oven and pour ½ carton of turkey stock over each pan.
- Put back in oven to finish cooking.

IT SMELLS READY: SIDE DISHES & APPETIZERS

Corrina's Caponata Siciliana
(serves 6–8)

This traditional Sicilian caponata is a family recipe that bursts with flavor! It can be made and served the same or following day. What's fun about this dish, is that it can be made to your family's liking! This means, if you really love olives, feel free to add more. If you don't like capers, go a little lighter or remove them entirely. It's usually presented on a toasted, thin crostini, which you can make from a baguette and toast. It is most often served as an appetizer and enjoyed by everyone!

INGREDIENTI

1 eggplant

Sicilian green olives (~10)

Black olives (~10)

1 T roasted red peppers

1 T capers

2 T white wine vinegar

1 garlic clove

½ yellow onion

1 T sugar

1 ½ cup crushed tomatoes

6 figs (qb)

Basil (to garnish)

Toast crostini (to serve)

Direzioni

- Sauté the finely chopped garlic and chopped onion in the olive oil until brown on low to medium heat.
- In separate pan, sauté cubed eggplant.
- Add the crushed tomatoes, capers, olives (halved), white wine vinegar, sugar, peppers, and fig to garlic and onions.
- Sauté and stir for a few minutes, then add fully cooked eggplant.
- Let it stand in a warm pan, stirring occasionally for about 1 hour.
- Serve on hot or cold on thin toasted crostini. Plate when ready to serve.

IT SMELLS READY: SIDE DISHES & APPETIZERS

ENJOY EVERY BITE: DESSERTS

Nonna Mary's Italian Biscotti
(makes 6–8 dozen cookies)

We believe Nonna Mary handmade over 1,000,000 of these cookies. Later in life, she began counting and documenting the thousands of biscotti she made. These biscotti, in one shape or another, were made for every birthday, baptism, first communion, confirmation, wedding, and funeral in the family and for friends. Nonna Mary also made dozens of these biscotti and shipped them to Mary's father when he served in Vietnam. And of course, they were made for you every time you went over her house, always eating at least one, and never leaving empty-handed.

Angela and Mary have since carried on this tradition with these cookies, learning how much love went into them as they shaped and twisted each cookies prior to baking them in the oven!

INGREDIENTI

6 eggs
1¾ cup sugar
1 cup melted butter
⅓ cup milk
1 T anise
2 T baking powder
7 cups flour

Frosting

2 cups powdered sugar
1 T anise
2 T soft butter
4 T milk
Sprinkles

Direzioni—Biscotti

- Beat 6 eggs until they are foamy, then add 1¾ cup of sugar.

- Mix well and add 1 cup of melted butter.

- Add ⅓ cup milk followed by 1 T of anise. (Substitute other flavors such as vanilla, almond, or lemon. Nonna Mary and Mary primarily made these biscotti that were vanilla-flavored; Angela makes them mostly with anise.)

- Add 2 T of baking powder.

- Add 7 cups of flour. For the best results, add each cup one at a time, incorporating and mixing well before adding the next.

- Cover and chill the dough for 3 hours.

- After chilled, let the dough sit for a few minutes so it's easier to work.

- Roll dough ¼- to ½-inch thick in long roll, about 12 inches long. Cut each biscotti on an angle about 2 inches long (see the picture on the back cover).

- Visit www.cugineincucina.com for additional pictures and details on this process.

- Bake for 10 minutes at 350°F. (**TIP:** Use parchment paper.)

Direzioni—Frosting

NOTE: For generous frosting coverage, double the frosting recipe.

- Blend 2 cups powdered sugar, 1 T of anise (or flavor of choice), 2 T of soft butter, and 4 T of milk. Use the same flavoring in the frosting as used in the cookie. For example, if you make anise cookies, use anise-flavored frosting; if you make vanilla cookies, use vanilla-flavored frosting.

- Dip the top of the cooled biscotti into the frosting and add nonpareil sprinkles on top while the frosting is still wet. Let sit to dry frosting. Nonna Mary used her finger to brush the frosting across the top, rather than dipping it.

ENJOY EVERY BITE: DESSERTS

Aunt Angie's Carrot (or Zucchini) Cake (serves 12)

INGREDIENTI

2 cups flour

2 tsp baking powder

1½ tsp baking soda

1 tsp salt

¾ cup oil

¾ cup brown sugar (packed)

4 eggs

2 cups grated carrots OR grated zucchini

Optional (zucchini): ½ cup of nuts; ½ cup raisins

Optional (carrot): ½ cup of nuts (walnuts or pecans); ½ cup raisins; ½ cup shredded coconut; 1 cup crushed pineapple (drained)

Frosting (carrot cake only)

1 cup softened butter

6 cups powdered sugar

16 oz. cream cheese (softened)

6 tsp vanilla

This cake—either the carrot version or the zucchini version—became a staple at Angela and Corrina's family dinners. It all started in their father's garden with a surplus of carrots and zucchini! Their mother took her cooking ingenuity and started playing around the kitchen. The next thing they knew, she not only made a great cake from scratch, but she also was able to make it so either ingredient (carrot or zucchini) was interchangeable! This cake was served mostly in the summer when the carrots and zucchini were in season. This homemade frosting adds great flavor to the carrot cake.

Direzioni

Cake

- Mix the flour, baking powder, baking soda, salt, and brown sugar in large bowl.
- Add in the oil and eggs and mix until combined.
- Add either the shredded carrot or zucchini.
- Add any of the optional ingredients (depending on which cake you are making).
- Pour zucchini cake mixture into one large or two small loaf pans, greased. OR
- Pour carrot cake mixture into a 10-inch round cake pan, greased.

- Bake at 350°F for 35–40 minutes until a toothpick comes out clean from the center.

TIP: Carrot cake may take a bit longer to cook all the way through. Keep checking it every 5 minutes until the toothpick comes out clean from the center. Let the cake cool completely prior to frosting.

Frosting

- Mix butter and powdered sugar in a bowl.
- Add the cream cheese and mix well (can use hand mixer).
- Add the vanilla.
- With a separate spoon, taste. If prefer sweeter, add ½ cup powdered sugar.

ENJOY EVERY BITE: DESSERTS

Mary's Strawberry Granita
(Italian Ice) (serves 4–6)

Mary prefers to stay on the healthier side of her recipes. She will sometimes substitute honey for simple syrup to keep the sweetness and use a natural ingredient. If you notice that your strawberries are ripe and very juicy, take advantage of the natural juices and add a little less simple syrup. Note: Substitute your favorite fruits as you please. You can also do an equal part mix, such as a blueberry-banana mix for more deliciousness!

INGREDIENTI

3 cups ripe strawberries

1 cup water

¾ cup sugar

2 T lemon juice

Direzioni

- Be sure your strawberries are washed well, then smash (or puree).
- Create a simple syrup by bringing water to a boil, then remove from heat and add the sugar. Stir until the sugar is dissolved and set aside to cool.
- Add mashed strawberries to cooled simple syrup, then add lemon juice (add more to taste, qb).
- Freeze in bowl or molds until firm.
- Serve frozen.

ENJOY EVERY BITE: DESSERTS

Angela's Cannoli Dip
(serves 6)

It's not every day that you get to share your heritage! Here, the traditional Sicilian cannoli is turned into a dip and served with a classic American cracker. This is a perfect dessert to bring to a party. Most people who try it for the first time want the recipe! You'll want to store the dip in the refrigerator and serve cold.

INGREDIENTI

- 1 cup heavy cream
- 8 oz. mascarpone
- 4 oz. cream cheese (softened)
- 16 oz. whole milk ricotta cheese (drained)
- 1 cup powdered sugar
- 4 tsp vanilla extract
- 1 tsp lemon zest
- 1 tsp orange zest
- 1 10 oz. bag of dark mini chocolate chips

Direzioni

Note: If you are unable to strain the ricotta overnight, add 2 teaspoons almond flour.

- Beat the whipping cream until you have stiff peaks.
- In a separate bowl, mix the mascarpone, cream cheese, ricotta cheese, powdered sugar, almond flour, and vanilla.
- With a rubber spatula, fold in the whipping cream, and mini chocolate chips.
- Scoop mixture into a serving bowl or onto a platter, then sprinkle zests on top.
- Serve with chocolate or honey graham crackers.

Tip

This dip can also be served with broken cannoli shells.

ENJOY EVERY BITE: DESSERTS

Mary's Bella Luna Cookie
(makes about 30 cookies)

This is an Italian-style moon pie. Mary and her mother were in the kitchen with a taste for something sweet, so they looked at the ingredients they had readily available. Shortly after, the Bella Luna was born! It's a baked ricotta-filled pastry shell that should be refrigerated in an airtight container and served cool. Dust with powdered sugar just before serving. It's been a party favorite—something unique, delicious, and with an Italian twist! Mary makes and sells these cookies under Ciao Down Italian Cookies, LLC.

INGREDIENTI

4 pie crusts

15 oz. ricotta cheese (drained overnight)

1 scant cup of powdered sugar

1 tsp vanilla

Direzioni

- Remove the pie crust (store bought is fine) from the refrigerator. It is easier to work with at room temperature.
- To make the filling, we do everything to taste (qb) and mix ricotta, powdered sugar, and vanilla well.
- Use a 3-inch diameter cookie cutter to cut each of the cookies. This will give you 7 or 8 cookies per pie crust.
- Scoop about 1 teaspoon of filling onto each of the cut-outs. It's better to have a little less filling than a little more in each piece—in case some of the filling escapes in the baking process!
- Fold the dough in half, and pinch the sides to ensure the filling is secure. You may want to use a fork and press firmly enough to make an imprint but don't push through the dough.
- Bake at 425°F for about 10–12 minutes (until golden).
- Once cooled, dust with powdered sugar before serving.

ENJOY EVERY BITE: DESSERTS

Measurements & Conversion Charts

Oven Temperature Conversion Chart

Fahrenheit	Centigrade	Description
475F	246C	Very Hot
450F	232C	Very Hot
425F	218C	Fairly Hot
400F	204C	Fairly Hot
375F	191C	Moderately Hot
350F	177C	Warm
325F	163C	Warm
300F	149C	Cool
275F	135C	Cool
250F	121C	Very Cool
225F	110C	Very Cool

Volume/Liquid Measurements

240 8 fl. oz.	1 US cup
300 10 fl. oz.	0.5 pint
425 15 fl. oz.	0.75 pint
480 16 fl. oz.	1 US pint
600 20 fl. oz.	1 pint
700 23 fl. oz.	1.25 pints
850 28 fl. oz.	1.5 pints
1 33 fl. oz.	1.75 pints

Volume/Liquid Measurements

1.25 ml.	1/4 teaspoon
2.5 ml.	1/2 teaspoon
5 ml.	1 level teaspoon
15 ml.	1 tablespoon (1/2 fl. oz.)
20 ml.	1 dessert spoon
30 ml.	1 fl. oz.
50 ml.	2 fl. oz.
59 ml.	1/4 US cup
74 ml.	1/4 UK cup
118 ml.	4 fl. oz. 1/2 US cup
150 ml.	0.5 (UK) pint 1/2 UK cup
200 ml.	0.66 pint

ml. is millilitres
fl. oz. is fluid ounce

Imperial Weights

1 kg.	2 lb. 3 oz.
1.25 kg.	2 lb. 12 oz.
1.5 kg.	3 lb. 5 oz.
1.75 kg.	3 lb. 14 oz.
2 kg.	4 lb. 6 oz.
2.25 kg.	4 lb. 15 oz.
2.5 kg.	5 lb. 8 oz.
2.75 kg.	6 lb. 1 oz.
3 kg.	6 lb. 10 oz.

1 US stick of butter is the equivalent to 1/4 lbs. (113.5 gm.)

Metric Weights

10 gm.	0.5 oz.
20 gm.	0.75 oz.
25 gm.	1 oz.
50 gm.	2 oz.
75 gm.	3 oz
110 gm.	4 oz.
150 gm.	5 oz.
175 gm.	6 oz.
200 gm.	7 oz.
225 gm.	8 oz.
250 gm.	9 oz.
275 gm.	9.5 oz.
300 gm.	10.5 oz.
350 gm.	12 oz.
375 gm.	13 oz.
400 gm.	14 oz.
425 gm.	15 oz.
450 gm.	1 lb. (pound)
500 gm.	1 lb. 2 oz.
700 gm.	1 lb. 9 oz.
750 gm.	1 lb. 10 oz.

Our Genealogy

Great grandparents Sam and Josephine

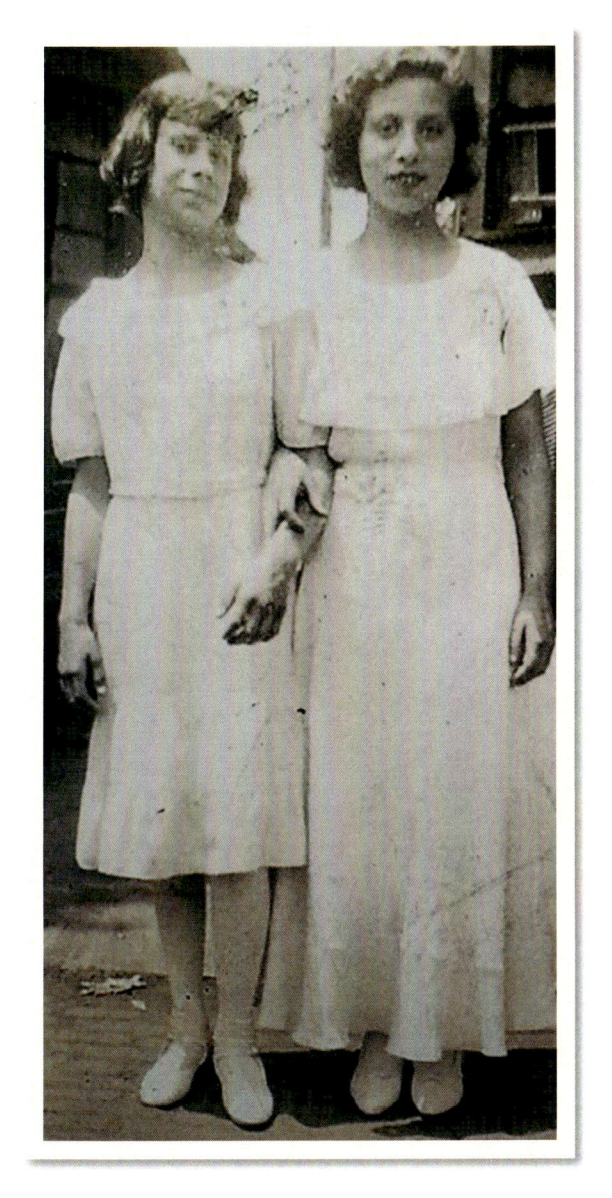

Nonna Mary (left) and Nonna Josie in First Communion dresses

OUR GENEALOGY   73

Nonna Josie with her father, Sam, on her wedding day

Nonna Josie and Nonno Massie on their wedding day

Nonna Mary with her father Sam on her wedding day (top)
Nonna Mary with Nonno Joe on their wedding day

76 DON'T CUT THE BASIL

Angela and Carmen on their wedding day

Josephine and Jim on their wedding day

OUR GENEALOGY 77

Nonna Mary and Nonna Josie with their siblings

Massie, Joe, Mary, Joey (sibling), and Josie eating homemade pizza

Nonna Josie

OUR GENEALOGY 79

Nonna Mary

Nonna Mary and Mary

OUR GENEALOGY   81

Nonna Mary, Mamacita, and Mary

Corrina and Angela holding a picture of their mother Angela and grandmother Josephine

OUR GENEALOGY

Angela (center) with her children, Isabella and Gianna

Corrina with her husband, Troy

OUR GENEALOGY 85

Corrina and Troy's children: Carmela, Antonella, and Dominic

DON'T CUT THE BASIL